Optimism for the New Millennium: Essential Life Skills for Today

Sibis Mouton, Ph.D

Optimism for the New Millennium:
Essential Life Skills for Today

ISBN book: 978-0-620-72677-1

ISBN ebook: 978-0-620-73402-8

Contents

Acknowledgements

In 2013 I approached the sportswear company Adidas to sponsor my life skills programme at Cape Peninsula University of Technology (CPUT) by providing a pair of running shoes every month for a semester. Students were instructed to write their names, along with an act of kindness they had performed, and place the slip in an Adidas box. The monthly prize was awarded to the student chosen in a lucky draw. I would like to thank Mr Adrian De Souza, head of marketing at Adidas, for coming through with the monthly prizes—not only in 2013, but in 2014 as well.

Adidas has kept me in shoes since 1987—right through my international career as a triathlete representing South Africa (1993–2004), and even afterwards. My thanks also to Gavin Cowley, who gave the initial nod to this sponsorship.

A word of thanks as well to my head of department at CPUT, Ms Ashaadia Kamalie, who permitted me to teach life skills to civil engineering students in CPUT's Extended Curriculum Programme. My HOD aptly described the course as the Adidas Boost Programme. I'm also thankful to my line manager, Mr Noor Armien, who has always supported the Life Skills Programme with great enthusiasm.

Last but not least, profound thanks to my patient editor, Jennifer Woodhull, who is a whiz with the English language and who has helped me tremendously to write everything in a better—and more English—way.

I begin this book with an essay by one of my 2013 students. The students were asked to describe what they had learnt from the Adidas Life Skills Programme. I posed the question, "What would you teach your little brother/sister, based on what you have learnt?" This response, by Mbalenhle Baloyi, appears in edited form. My comment on the returned essay: "A very good essay, Mbalenhle. Hope you have a blessed life and reach all your goals!"

Prologue

A Student's-eye View of the Life Skills Programme

The Life Skills Programme directed by Dr Sibis Mouton served as a fundamental skill endorsement in my life. I got an opportunity to acquire knowledge and skills of different sorts, and to improve the ones I already had. I got to learn about my brain and how it operates. This enabled me to gain control over certain feelings that I previously could not control, and helped me solve certain conflicts and misunderstandings with other people in a peaceful yet orderly way, where we both left the scene satisfied and with a clean conscience.

I also got to learn about the power of visualisation, and about living life by design rather than letting circumstances decide my day's plans and emotions for me. Instead, I learned to actually make my own plans and decide how I would feel about my experiences. I learned about the importance of decision-making, and that the choices we make daily reveal who we really are and determine what we'll become in future. Now I know it is necessary to think further before making any choice.

I got to learn about living life with purpose, using the four agreements: always doing my best, not assuming, not taking anything personally, and being impeccable with my word. I learned about the importance of having and knowing my skills and values, because they define who I really am; and that the best way to get tasks done is by rewarding myself after I complete each one.

I also got to learn about a whole lot of other things, like knowing my personality traits and life purposes; time management; health and eating exercises that can help me live a long, fulfilling, and happy life; and the ten virtues and terrible ten things one needs to eliminate from one's life. And finally, last but not least, my favourite: *the new consciousness.* This helped me understand myself better, and motivated me to improve my life by changing my views on certain things.

Applying the fifty acts of kindness was actually fun and reviving, something I'll carry out for life.

I would most definitely recommend this programme for future students because it helps with mental, spiritual, academic, and emotional growth. It will help them understand and deal with how and why certain things happen. I feel that this is an essential skill for future engineers.

—Mbalenhle Baloyi

Chapter 1
Tough and Resilient—
The Way of the Warrior

Optimism is the tendency to believe, expect, or hope that things will turn out well. Can we still be optimistic today? My answer is yes—if we can yield to whatever is in front of us without resistance. The belief that there is a perfect plan behind all the chaos we see in life today can be an immense solace. In order to carry this positive attitude, however, we need the resilience of the warrior.

I once read the remarkable story of two hunters on the trail of Cape buffalo. From my own experience of game watching, I know that the buffalo is one of the most feared animals in the wild—especially lonely old bulls. In this hunting story, the hunters shot a buffalo through the heart and then a further six times—but it was still coming at its tormentors. Eventually, the bull flopped down about ten metres from them, apparently stone dead. Relieved, one of the hunters moved forward to take a closer look at the resilient animal. The buffalo rose, killed the hunter, and then finally dropped dead!

That animal was clearly a warrior, though not necessarily a peaceful one! The tradition of the "peaceful warrior" has a long and venerable history in Eastern cultures. Dan Millman is just one Western author who has made this powerful idea accessible to us. His 1980 book, *Way of the Peaceful Warrior,* follows the adventures of a champion gymnast who discovers his inner strength by coming to know his heart.

The Toughness of the Warrior

Growing up in Africa, I was regaled with war tales of Zulu *impis* (armies). It is said that King Shaka made his warriors run over thorn fields to harden them.

It seems to me that young people used to be much tougher. My 83-year-old swim coach, Mr Brian Button, grew up in Kimberley, an important South African diamond-mining city. Mr Button recalls as a boy having had to wear shorts right through the year—even on this near-desert region's typically cold, frosty mornings.

I was glad to hear that at the prestigious private Grey College in Bloemfontein, boys can still choose whether to wear long or short pants through the cold winter. Apparently, those boys raised on farms continue to wear shorts. For them, it is a sign of toughness—and probably a matter of pride, too!

My Life Skills Programme at the Cape University of Technology included a physical period, about once a month. I took students to the university's tartan track and warmed them up with stretching and a bit of running. Then I timed them as they ran a kilometre (2,5 laps). The students' initial times ranged from three minutes twenty-seven seconds to ten minutes twenty-two seconds. In running circles a time of four minute a kilometre is respectable.

I was surprised to notice that some of these students really did not know how to run. South Africa's new education programme has made physical education redundant; this could be just one effect. Personally, I feel that dropping physical education was a bad idea. Students are better learners when they are physically active.

The anecdotes mentioned above stress physical toughness, certainly a characteristic of the true warrior. But it isn't the only kind of toughness the warrior needs. Most peak performance books stress the ability to consistently perform toward the upper range of one's talent and skill, *regardless of circumstances*. Paavo Nurmi, a Finnish athlete who won nine gold medals at the 1920, 1924, and 1928 Olympics (and set twenty-five world records running distances ranging from 1500 m to 20 km) was known as "the Flying Finn". One of his famous utterances is: "Mind is everything; muscle—pieces of rubber. All that I am, I am because of my mind."

Another tough hero of the past was the Ethiopian Abebe Bikila, who won the 1960 Olympic marathon in Rome, running the whole 42 km barefoot! A week before the 1964 Olympics in Tokyo, Bikila underwent surgery for acute appendicitis. But he showed up for the marathon and won another gold medal!

The Secret Ingredient

In the animated movie *Kung Fu Panda*, the hero's dad – a duck – keeps referring to the secret ingredient in his soup. Eventually it turns out there is no secret ingredient. When one believes one's soup is special, *it is special*!

Following this strategy, I ask: *What is the secret ingredient of a life full of optimism?* We will only be optimistic if we understand the art of letting go; when we can really yield to what is in front of us. Having the ability to accept what life is giving us and look at things positively means we can manifest a positive attitude in any situation.

At his public talks, Prof Tim Noakes, the world famous Capetonian sports scientist and protagonist of the Banting diet, enjoys showing footage of "his" University of Cape Town rugby team. The video shows the team winning an intervarsity game at the very last minute. Noakes's secret ingredient was that the team believed they were going to win. Kung Fu Panda made a similar discovery when his accomplishment as the greatest of fighters gave him the magical ability to open a secret scroll. The scroll was completely blank. All Kung Fu Panda needed was to believe that he was the greatest fighter—and he was!

Few of us dream of being the world's greatest fighter, but most of us long for a life of joy and peace. Could it be that believing we already have it, is the secret ingredient necessary for an optimistic attitude?

I got the feeling that my young Life Skills students, rather than being proactive, positive, and active, were waiting for things to happen to them. John F. Kennedy, the thirty-fifth president of the United States, made the following memorable statement: "Ask not what your country can do for you; ask what you can do for your country". I wanted to tell my students, "Ask not what this world can do for you; ask what you can do for this world". This inspirational suggestion sums up the secret of a joyful life.

Fifty Acts of Kindness[1]

To help my students on the journey of the proactive warrior, I gave them a list of fifty acts of kindness they could choose to perform. Each completed act was written down and dropped into a box. The lucky student whose act of kindness came up in a monthly draw won a pair of brand new Adidas running shoes. As you can see, I literally bribed them to be kind!

It has been documented that performing acts of kindness increases our levels of oxytocin, a hormone associated with a feeling of well-being. Getting our oxytocin levels up gives us a whole lot more than just a good feeling: apparently, the hormone is cardio-protective. It prevents hardening of the arteries, dilates our blood vessels, reduces blood pressure, encourages wound healing, helps in the construction of foetal hearts, and may even help in the regeneration of damaged heart muscle.[2] And that's in addition to the spiritual benefits we derive from being kind and considerate!

Oxytocin is produced when we connect with each other. Not surprisingly, many studies are now showing that positive relationships are good for our health. Apparently, people in healthy relationships are at a lower risk of heart disease than single people are.

---

[1] This idea, and the list that follows, are drawn from David Hamilton's book *Why Kindness is Good for You.*

[2] David Hamilton, "Wired for Kindness", *Odyssey* Magazine.

Here is that list of fifty suggestions for (random) acts of kindness. If any of them inspire you, I encourage you to go right out and see how it feels to actually do them. The oxytocin benefits alone are worth the experiment!

1. Write a thank-you card to someone.

2. Offer to carry an elderly person's shopping.

3. Allow someone to go in front of you in the supermarket queue.

4. Give someone a compliment.

5. Buy an extra parking ticket and leave it on the parking meter for the next person to find.

6. Pay for an extra pair of cinema tickets and ask the server to give them to someone they feel would appreciate them.

7. Leave R50 at the till of a coffee shop and ask the manager to use it to pay for everyone's coffees until it is used up.

8. Tell someone in a shop or restaurant that they are doing a great job.

9. When someone cuts you off on the road, smile and wave them on.

10. Send a card to a former school teacher or university professor and tell them how much they influenced your life.

11. Buy some food for a homeless person.

12. Use an online supermarket service to send a box of food to a family you know could use it.

13. Join a charity as a regular volunteer.

14. Offer to look after a friend or family member's children for a few hours.

15. Phone someone up on their birthday and sing "Happy Birthday" to them.

16.	Offer your seat on the bus or train to an elderly person.

17.	Be a friend to someone in need.

18.	Make a donation to a charity.

19.	Sponsor a child.

20.	Foster or adopt a child from an orphanage.

21.	Buy a large box of cakes and pastries and give them out on the street.

22.	Take out an advert in a newspaper, wishing everyone a nice day.

23.	Give your loved one breakfast in bed.

24.	Buy a gift for someone.

25.	Buy lunch or dinner for someone who is short of money.

26.	If someone is giving out leaflets on the street, take one, smile and thank them for offering it to you. Make a point of reading it.

27.	If you are given too much change, take it back to the shop.

28.	Give blood.

29.	Write a letter of gratitude to someone who has influenced your life, hand deliver it, and read it out to them.

30.	If you are getting coffee for yourself in the office, offer to get one for your colleagues—or just surprise someone with a coffee on your return.

31.	Send chocolates at Christmas to a company that has provided you with good service.

32.	Send flowers to an elderly person.

33.	Visit an elderly person and listen to their stories.

34. Find out what a loved one or friend really wants and provide it for them, if possible.

35. Buy a book for someone.

36. Tell someone they look great.

37. Throw a party for someone who deserves some appreciation.

38. Offer to tidy an elderly neighbour's garden.

39. Offer to do some shopping for someone who's not able to do it themselves.

40. Take someone on a night out.

41. When a new person joins the company you work for or moves into your street, make them feel welcome by taking them to lunch.

42. Hold a door open for someone.

43. Slip some money into the purse or pocket of someone who needs it so that when they find it, they think they must have misplaced it.

44. Write a poem or song for someone.

45. Search out inspirational or funny videos on YouTube, or other inspirational or funny material, and send it to someone who needs it.

46. Pay a kindness forward. If someone does something kind for you, do something kind for someone else, to carry the kindness forward.

47. Do a chore for someone that you know they hate doing.

48. Give someone a hug for no reason.

49. Make peace with a troublesome neighbour or work colleague, even if you're in the right—it'll be good for both of you.

50. Take a loaf of bread to a pond and feed the ducks.

Another Ingredient

Warriors should not only be tough and kind; they should also know what their passion is. During the so-called Cold War of the previous millennium, we grew up with the term "the Iron Curtain". This was the curtain dividing the Communist world from the Western democracies. The Berlin Wall literally divided that city in two, with Communism practised on the eastern side and capitalist democracy on the western side. An ex-Communist who escaped Poland when she was sixteen and ended up in Greece made this distinction between the two ideologies: "Communism was really nice: we all had houses, we all had work, and we all had a car. *But we did not have a dream!*"

It was Dr Martin Luther King Jr who uttered the famous words, "I have a dream". In a speech delivered on August 28, 1963 to 250 thousand civil rights supporters at the Lincoln Memorial in Washington, DC, Dr King repeated this sentence eight times. But few remember the content of his famous dream. "I have a dream", Dr King said, "that my four little children will one day live in a nation where they will not be judged by the colour of their skin, but by the content of their character." This aspiration perfectly expresses my own deeply held wish for our planet.

A friend told me this delightful story. During a romantic sojourn in Amsterdam, he and his wife were enjoying coffee at a corner shop. It was a lovely spring day in this beautiful city. Opposite them, students were emerging from a university where they had just received their degrees. One of the graduates sat with a friend at the next table.

At that moment, the advocate and his wife noticed a cat chasing butterflies in the midst of busy traffic. They expressed their concern that the cat would be run over; but the new graduate surprised them with this refreshing remark: "Let the cat be. I would love to die while catching my dream!" My friend wasn't surprised to discover that this young woman's degree was in psychology.

Priming the Pump

I recently visited the Victoria Falls for the second time in my life, joining four others on a two-hour horse trail through the adjacent reserve. Our guide made us stop at a herd of buffaloes. I felt a bit uncomfortable, but the guide immediately put my mind at ease. Apparently the buffaloes see only the horse, and not the rider; so we were well camouflaged in the presence of these dangerous animals.

In this instance, the art of camouflage worked well for us. But can we always see through the clever disguises of modern life, with its materialistic seductions and compelling technologies? Can we stay tough and resilient and optimistic in the face of all that? Can we believe in ourselves? I think of that moment of safety on my horse, amongst the wild buffaloes. Like a good rider, we can hold our seat and remain tall in the saddle. Then we can faithfully pursue our individual dreams, surrender to what life dishes up for us, and stay optimistic about whatever outcome we meet.

South Africa has many water pumps, especially in the drier areas of our country. Some of the older pumps work on the principle of "priming": you first introduce a little water to prime the pump, which encourages the rest of the water to follow. So if you want water, first add water!

The same principle applies to living a stress-free and victorious life. When we are optimistic and sure about our dreams, we prime our internal pump with peace—the inner peace that comes from surrendering to a bigger plan, but with clear intentions. From there, external peace is sure to follow.

IDEAS:

ACTIONS:

Chapter 2
In Search of a Little Madness—
or, Is Anybody's Religion Necessarily
Right or Wrong?

Let's look at Adam and Eve. Is this Abrahamic creation story a total myth, or does it contain a grain of truth about Paradise? I can tell you this: if Adam and Eve had been Chinese, we would still be in Paradise. They would have eaten that snake!

And what about the pot of gold at the end of the rainbow? Are we doomed to eternally search for something we will never find?

"I guess if I want the rainbow, I have to put up with the rain"—these wise words have been attributed to Dolly Parton. And as it turns out, I am quite glad Adam and Eve did not swallow that snake, because I now have the opportunity to experience life with all of its polarities: the agony and the ecstasy, the rain and the sunshine. I can be mad and I can have reason. I can truly be alive!

To be passionate about the polarities of life is to live life fully. It means one is optimistic and can experience all that life has to offer.

While doing some research on the many mystics who have walked the earth, I came upon the following story. Saint Teresa of Avila (1515–1582) is probably the most famous female Christian mystic. She was a feisty Spanish nun of Jewish descent, and apparently of great physical beauty. She initiated a reform of Carmelite convents and monasteries, calling for a return to silent prayer and humility. Teresa was said to be endowed with a very quick wit and a stunning sense of humour.

Known for her love of partridge, St Teresa was spotted in the convent kitchen one day devouring a whole bird. The nuns were astounded to see their supreme abbess reveling in this gastronomic delight. St Teresa's alleged response to their shocked exclamations: "When I fast, I fast; and when I eat partridge, I eat partridge!" This lovely story illustrates the balance of the mystical life.

Zorba the Greek, in the wonderful book of the same name by Nikos Kazantzakis, shows a similar passion for life. Passion comes when we are in perfect balance and when we have learnt to stay in the present moment—to enjoy the moment given to us with gusto and relish.

The Sanskrit term for the soul, *Ātman*, really means "happiness", or bliss itself. Indian mystic Hazrat Inayat Khan (1882–1927) taught that it is not that happiness *belongs* to the soul; rather, the soul itself *is* happiness. According to Khan, real happiness comes to those who have discovered the fountain of happiness within their own hearts. Until we find that fountain, he says, nothing will give us real happiness.

The mystical Sufi poet Rumi (1207–1273) is currently the most widely read poet in the United States. He wrote that the whole world is inside us. There are "wild forces" within us, which Rumi identifies with love itself. To find that love within is to dance in ecstasy. Rumi found this love through his spiritual master and beloved friend, Shams of Tabriz. Like Rumi, St John of the Cross (1542–1591) discovered his happiness in his "Beloved". In a mystical poem he proclaimed, "I now see my Beloved everywhere".

It is the desire for, and eventual union with, the Beloved within us that will make our souls dance. The myth of the lost Paradise tells us that we were kicked out of Eden and consequently have to live our lives separated from the Divine. So sadly, we go looking for Paradise somewhere else, somewhere out there, outside ourselves.

Alberto Villoldo, an American psychiatrist, relates an experience he had while working with the shamans of the Amazon Forest. One day an old medicine woman instructed him to walk into the forest. As soon as he stepped among the trees, birds and insects stopped singing. There was dead silence! The medicine woman attributed this silence to Alberto's belief in our exile from the Garden of Eden, which made him feel separated from God and nature.

Alberto cunningly smeared himself with the fat of a boa constrictor, thinking that maybe now the forest animals and insects wouldn't recognise him as human. No luck! As he walked back in again there was just dead silence. Alberto reports that it took him ten years of walking in the forest before the birds and insects kept on singing. That was how long it took him to finally learn to feel at one with nature—to feel connected with all that is.

Once, on a late winter afternoon in Hermanus, I saw a beautiful and perfect rainbow. Hermanus is a lovely seaside town on the southern coast of South Africa. One end of the rainbow sprouted from the green mountain and the other plunged into the sea over Walker Bay, where a couple of whales were playing in the water. At that moment it struck me that the mountain end of the rainbow is like the self, solid and unchangeable. We are stuck with ourselves! The other end of the rainbow is our relationship with others, more changeable and mobile. Some people drift in and out of our lives; some stay for a lifetime, others just for a season. The sea side of the rainbow can also be its stormy side, as stormy as the ocean itself can be. For it is through our difficult dances with others that we really grow and become wiser.

The beauty of the connecting rainbow and its seven vivid colours is the bridge between us and others, signifying the presence of our eternal divinity: the Light that is within each of us. The Divine/the Force/the Universe—however you think of it—is that bridge that connects us with others and with ourselves.

When we are in love with beauty and we realise that this creative power is the source of everything—of our arms moving, of our legs walking—we can start living life with the balance of the saints. Then we have vanquished the snake and allowed the Divine to come to the shores of our soul. Then Ātman, our soul, will experience that bliss that all the mystics talk about.

If we dig hard enough for the pot of gold, we will find it. But we must look for that spark within ourselves, not under the arch of the rainbow. If we find the gold before the end of our life journey, we have found everlasting life.

The Chinese mystic and Zen master Huang Po, who died in 850 CE, reported that enlightenment comes in a flash. This flash of enlightenment is actually the only real death we experience: the death of the self and the surrender to the Source. So the death of self is the birth of bliss. Woody Allen said, "I'm not afraid of death; I just don't want to be there when it happens". But we had better be present for this momentous event!

Eat the apple, forget about the snake. Live with zest and a touch of madness every day. Do something wild and get in touch with your real self. Take a few minutes—or hours— every day to escape the dull routine of daily disciplined living. Go and dance naked in your back yard in the light of the full moon with the wet grass under your bare feet. Live like Zorba: "Man needs a little madness or else he never dares cut the rope and be free."

Live life fully, even if you get rained on. The rain, inevitably, is the source of that beautiful rainbow. Do the fasting, by all means, but bring in the feast as well. Practise discipline, but bring in a touch of wildness. Plunge into action, but also take time to enjoy some contemplation and solitude. This way, we can truly live in Paradise, even though the snake is still amongst us! Optimism in this millennium is the spontaneous flow of love: love for everyone and everything, regardless of their religion or beliefs.

Tessa Bielecki, a former Carmelite nun who now lectures in Christian mysticism at the University of Colorado, says that the very heart of mysticism lies in "the dynamic interplay of the seemingly opposing polar forces; living the agony and the ecstasy, the masculine and the feminine, the fasting and the feasting. Life is not either/or, it is *both/and*". Working with this wisdom, each one of us can be a mystic.

St John of the Cross was 25 when he met St Teresa of Avila, then in her fifties. Her wonderful spiritual power had a great transformational effect on him. These two saints were said to really love one another, in the purest sense. It's said that when Teresa was in conversation with John she levitated, spontaneously rising up into the air.

The church persecuted St Teresa for her liberating ideas. At 67, after a year of imprisonment, she died and was buried in Alba de Tormes. A year after her death, some of her disciples felt that she would have preferred to have been buried in Avila, her birthplace. When her year-old corpse was exhumed, it was found to be completely intact, and it emitted a wonderful fragrance. This was one of the reasons why, despite her clash with the traditional church, St Teresa was declared a saint.

I close this essay with the following beautiful poem by St Teresa. May you experience Paradise in all its fullness here and now; dance with the snake (which is, most fortunately, not Chinese); and eat the whole partridge in one shot! And my opinion is that nobody's religion is necessarily right or wrong!

Laughter Came from Every Brick

Just these two words He spoke changed my life,
"Enjoy Me".

What a burden I thought I was to carry—a crucifix, as did He.
Love once said to me "I know a song, would you like to hear it?"

And laughter came from every brick in the street and from every pore in the sky.
After a night of prayer, He changed my life when He sang "Enjoy Me".

Life Skills Packet

The Life Skills Programme included no religious content of any kind. However, students were encouraged to think of a full human life as comprising four components: physical, mental, emotional and spiritual.

IDEAS:

ACTIONS:

Chapter 3
In Pursuit of the Present

So much has been written about living in the present moment. Eckhardt Tolle calls it *the power of now* (also the title of his bestselling book). Dreams can only be realised when the spiritual warrior lives by choice and not by default. The way of the warrior is to take an active role in directing and structuring her/his life. This means that we are totally in the moment and make immediate decisions.

In some of my life coaching courses, I ask clients to choose their top four values, and then to write down three aligning activities that support those values. We invariably make our choices at each stage of life based on what we really value. So whether I go on a 100 km bike ride or attend a friend's birthday party this Sunday will depend on my values at that time.

Then I have my clients complete a goal sheet, scoring themselves from 0 to 10 under the following headings:

- ❖ Mental and Educational
- ❖ Spiritual and Ethical
- ❖ Financial and Career
- ❖ Social and Cultural
- ❖ Physical and Health
- ❖ Family and Home

Finally, they write down three goals that they would like to achieve in the next five years.

Willie Jollie, American motivational speaker and author of the popular book *It Only Takes a Minute to Change Your Life*, gives the following tips for reaching our goals:

1. Identify what you really want.

2. Write it down. Be specific.

3. Read your goals three times every day.

4. Set a date for accomplishing them.

5. Think of them often.

6. Dream and imagine great results.

7. Develop a plan of action.

8. Take three actions every day towards your goals.

9. Stay positive.

10. Most important of all—act as though you have already achieved your dream.

Live by Intention

When our intentions are clear, we are actually living in the moment; we are living life by design. We are taking charge. We are purposeful, and not easily swayed by whatever wind may arise in our lives.

In an inspiring article (see "Further Reading"), Brian Parsley urges business leaders to see their purpose as an anchor. Once you know what your purpose is—perhaps the intention for your business to grow and thrive—you drop anchor, and never sway from your chosen course. This invariably makes life easier to handle. Parsley encourages leaders to act with determination, which naturally inspires others to follow suit and builds the leader's own confidence.

Another contemporary international teacher, Dr Bruce Lipton, says that the secret of life is to harness the mind to promote growth. When we aren't growing, he suggests, we're living in fear of a future that actually does not exist! Our bodies respond to such thoughts: our cells feel our feelings within us. When we feed our cells with fear, they contract rather than expanding. Cells can only function optimally when our thinking processes are positive. They naturally answer the call to optimism, which prompts them to regenerate and become healthier.

I once climbed the famous Wolf Cracks in the Cederberg, seventeen years after having done it for the first time. To my dismay, I was unable to remember the route through the third crack. In my defence, I must say there had been a landslide some years previously. Anyhow, I was suddenly confronted with a big rock that barred the way. I could not recall this obstacle at all. When memory becomes vague like this, we tend to replace it by painting our own picture of the past. The past becomes our own creation, bearing little resemblance to what actually happened. In other words, *the past as we understand it doesn't exist*.

Eckhardt Tolle points out that nobody has as yet planted their flag on the future, claiming to have discovered it. So if the future hasn't yet come into being and the past is unreal, should we not be content and peaceful in the present, as we see the natural world doing? All around us, nature is in an ever-creative mode. Plants and animals are simply enjoying the moment, always growing or flowering. It has been like this for millennia. There is an essentially bigger Force than ourselves at work.

In the epic futuristic movie, *Avatar,* inhabitants of the planet Pandora honoured the great works of Spirit in the form of the natural world. Through their trust in this greater power, the protagonist's prayers were answered. The invaders from Earth had no regard for the beauty of Pandora's natural environment, blindly destroying both it and the harmonious family life of the planet's inhabitants. This greedy, materialistic attitude was in complete contrast to the spiritual outlook of Pandora's people. In the end, all of the creatures on the planet united to defeat the invaders.

By honouring the natural world, as did the fictional Pandorans, we can keep coming back to the present moment. Only here can we realise the richness of a normal existence that is free of the constant compulsion to acquire things. Without fear of the non-existent future and no regrets about the unreal past, we can thoroughly enjoy the gifts of the moment, the ever-present *now*!

Practical Techniques for Enriching Your Present Moment

The following exercises were part of my Life Skills Programme. I encourage you to try them out—you may find them as helpful and inspiring as many of my students did!

At the start of this session, I had the students to gather in groups of four to contemplate Don Miguel Ruiz's "Four Agreements":

1. Be impeccable with your word.
2. Don't take anything personally.
3. Don't make assumptions.
4. Always do your best.

I asked the students to discuss what each of these agreements meant to them.

Next, we began working with the Life Skills Packet developed by the Breakthru Institute in Florida, where I received my training as a behavioural kinesiologist.

Life Skills

Identify the life skills you currently have and use by placing an "H" (have) in front of the life skill. Place a "W" (wish to have) in front of those you would like to possess.

	Anticipates		Manages
	Asks		Organises
	Builds		Plans
	Coaches		Proactive
	Communicates		Problem-solver
	Compassionate		Productive
	Contributes		Resourceful
	Creative		Sensual
	Discovers		Unstoppable
	Empathetic		Visionary
	Enrolling		Willing
	Facilitates		Wise
	Honest		Intuitive
	Innovative		Judgement
	Integrates		Leadership

Values

From the list below, select and prioritise the four most essential values in your life. If you don't find your values here, make up your own.

_______ Comfort

_______ Communication

_______ Contribution

_______ Creativity

_______ Curiosity

_______ Freedom

_______ Honesty

_______ Humour

_______ Independence

_______ Intimacy

_______ Joy

_______ Order

_______ Participation

_______ Peace

_______ Perfection

_______ Pleasure

_______ Power

_______ Recognition

_______ Spirituality/God

Rewards

These are your rewards for applying yourself to your goals. What "turns you on"? Select twenty-five items from the list below (or add your own).

Adventure		Inventing		Skydiving	
Rugby/Football		Kite Flying		Sunbathing	
Basketball		Massage		Surprises	
Being touched		Movies		Swimming	
Board games		Museums		Talking	
Boating		Music		Telling stories	
Bowling		Parks		Tennis	
Camping		Partying		TV	
Church		Pets		Travelling	
Classes		Picnics		Plays	
Concerts		Praying		Woodwork	
Crafts		Reading		Writing	
Dancing		Running		Yoga	
Decorating		Sculpting		Hiking	
Doodling		Sewing		DVDs	
Fixing		Sex/romance		Computers	
Giving		Shopping		Golf	

Exploring Your Life Purpose

1. If you were given £ 1,000,000,000 (one billion pounds) and were told you only had six months to live, what would you do and how would you spend your money?

2. Imagine you had the option of specifying what you wanted to be remembered for on your tombstone, and by whom. What would your tombstone say?

Remembered by:

Remembered for:

Personality Traits (Examples)

Use the following list to help you generate twenty personality traits that describe you. Select your five favourites and record them.

Sense of humour	Loyal
Self-love	Supportive
Self-esteem	Energetic
Empathy	Positive
Caring	Sexual
Loving	Happy
Responsible	Peaceful
Determined	Committed
Honest	Courageous
Persistent	Risk taker
Love of family	Curious
Desire to serve	Freedom loving
Great teacher	

Life Purposes (Examples)

The following are examples of life purposes that some people have discovered.

to enable	to inspire	to challenge
to awaken	to help	to produce
to direct	to understand	to counsel
to achieve	to master	to empower
to ignite	to journey	to seek
to participate	to relate	to listen
to synthesise	to intuit	to befriend
to organise	to negotiate	to validate
to create	to share	to energise
to teach	to heal	to liberate
to support	to love	to enhance
to enlighten	to accept	to design
to manage	to plan	to coach

My Ideal World

Writing in the present tense, complete the following sentence with your vision of an ideal world:

The purpose of my life is ....

IDEAS:

ACTIONS:

Chapter 4
Fear—The Other Side of the Thorn

Zen Buddhist master Thich Nhat Hahn said in one of his many books that "true happiness can only exist when fear is no longer there". In the course of my work as a behavioural kinesiologist, counselling many people each year, the truth of this saying has really sunk in. I have noticed that most of my clients' fears stem from some past experience. Once we have tracked down the originating event, we can talk about and view it in a different way.

This is exactly what happened with two young women who both came to see me with the same problem: they were too scared to drive. By using the method I've described, they were able to release this fear. One woman's fear stemmed from an event that happened when she was only five. Both of them are now happily driving around!

An older lady living on my street was very impressed with my fondness for swimming in the sea. She never does so herself any more, she told me, having been carried away by the current long ago at Ballito Bay in KwaZulu-Natal. I am sure there are incidents in my own past that make me fearful in certain situations, but nowadays I try to be fearless. I subscribe to the philosophy of that student in Amsterdam who said, "I would love to die while catching my dream!"

We all experience fearful reactions in our personal relationships. How can we handle them? At the Freedom Course I attended at the Breakthru Institute in Florida, I learned that the word FEAR really stands for "False Evidence Appearing Real". Applying this approach, we can see how thoroughly advertisers manipulate us into spending our money, based on our fears. To be totally free from fear is a challenge to us all.

Walking the White Rhino Trail

I had an opportunity to look directly at my own fear while
hiking on the unforgettable White Rhino Trail in the Umfolozi
Reserve, KwaZulu-Natal.

Our group of five adventurers left our kombi (VW bus) and
the base camp and, heavily laden with backpacks, food, and
sleeping gear, put our safety in the hands of our two Zulu
guides, Mandla and Jabulani. After scrambling downhill for five
minutes we took off our shoes and waded through a muddy
White Umfolozi River, where crocodiles abound. Although
Mandla guided us through the shallow part of the river, we
nevertheless felt uneasy. We had not yet discovered that our
able guides had forgotten to pack soap and coffee; nor that
the seven of us had just one toilet roll between us for our five
days in the wilderness!

The wilderness, for me, meant sitting high on the rocks
overlooking the Black Umfolozi River and watching a herd of
more than two hundred elephants cavorting in the water as
they crossed leisurely to the other side. It meant stories
around the campfire in the evenings or during our tea (alas,
no coffee) breaks during day hikes through the bush.

A story that particularly struck me was that of the *wag 'n
bietjie bos* ("wait-a-minute bush") and its significance in Zulu
culture. The bush in question has two thorns, one straight and
the other hooked. It is notorious for its stopping power—
especially if you're in a hurry and get hooked properly.
Disentangling its grip takes a while!

The Nguni people call this thorn bush "the tree of life"; its
scientific name is *ziziphus mucronata*. In the Zulu tradition, a
branch of this bush is used to take the spirit of a dead person
back to its home so it can rest in peace. A family member
must take a branch to where the person died, hook the spirit
with the curly thorn and then take it home. If this involves a
voyage by plane, train, or taxi, the family member must buy a
seat for the spirit next to him/her and put the branch on the

empty seat. If this is not done, according to Zulu folklore, ill luck will follow the family member and the spirit will not rest in peace.

A necessary aspect of this hiking experience was that of taking turns to be on watch at night to protect our fellow hikers from prowling wild animals. Each of the five of us had to stand watch for an hour and a half every night. I got the first watch our first night out, at a relatively early hour. By the fourth night, though, I was roused from my hard and uncomfortable bed on the rocks at two o'clock.

Part of the job was to keep the fire alive. I also had to walk about with a torch every five minutes to look for interlopers. During these dark hours, the mind can play a lot of games. Every creaking twig serves to unnerve you in the darkness of the enveloping bush. On the fourth night, I heard a mighty roar from the king of animals, the fearsome lion. Following a second roar that sounded as though it was about fifty metres away, I was about to waken Mandla (both our guides carried guns) when he turned over and said, "Don't worry, he is just greeting his brother. They are about a kilometre away."

I have no idea what we would have done had a herd of those big elephants decided to visit our campsite on the rocky edge of the gorge!

Dr David Hawkins, the late psychiatrist and director of the Sedona Spiritual Centre for Research, produced a series of audio programmes called *The Office Tapes*. On one entitled "Fear, Anxiety and Worry", he shares his technique for dealing with fear. *Do not resist the fear,* Dr Hawkins advises. *Be like a willow tree, bend with the wind; surrender*. Dr Hawkins and his research team developed a system of calibrating various life energies, summarised in a framework he calls the Consciousness Map. The more suffering and contraction associated with a given energy, the lower its score. By the same token, those energies that support health, harmony, and spiritual development score the highest. Dr Hawkins describes the Consciousness Map in detail in his book *Power versus Force*.

His own encounter with a rattlesnake while hiking in the mountains of Sedona, Arizona, perfectly illustrates his approach to working with fear. Dr Hawkins tells us that he opened the door of a mountain hut to encounter a huge rattlesnake, poised to strike. He knew he had split seconds to save his life. Instead of reacting in fear, Dr Hawkins completely surrendered to the moment. He felt an incredible peace, as if an invisible Presence presided over him and the rattlesnake—as if they were one. He said the energy field around them must have been near to 600 (the level of Enlightenment). Dr Hawkins reports that he could feel the Presence of the Divine in his togetherness with the rattlesnake. Nothing happened; both he and the rattlesnake were caught in this peaceful, non-threatening state. If he had reacted in fear, the rattlesnake would certainly have struck him.

Most of us think that we can avoid what we fear by being hypervigilant and self-protective. But as it turns out, this tactic does not help us eliminate our fear—it actually hinders us. On the scale of consciousness developed by Dr Hawkins and his research team, the energy field of Anxiety scores very low. In reality, fear attracts the very thing that we fear.

Many of us are especially governed by fear when it comes to relationship issues. We take refuge in our heads, coming up with the most wonderful reasons why we should not surrender to the field of Love—not surprisingly, among the highest scorers on Dr Hawkins's scale. We are scared to open our hearts because we fear pain and rejection. But it is impossible to truly give the gift of intimacy unless our hearts are open. Only then we can be genuinely vulnerable and grow in love. Grace, an aspect of the unfathomable intelligence of the universe, can only be bestowed on us when our hearts are open.

Fear stifles us. It keeps us from experiencing the fullness and abundance of life—which is exactly what makes us feel alive. The world is in need of people who are alive, who live and love effortlessly. President Theodore Roosevelt once used this analogy in a speech: *If you have a piece of string, you cannot make it go forward by pushing it, by using force; it just crumples up. But if you draw it, it follows where your hand is leading.*

The truth is that everyone needs our love. By giving with an open heart, we keep the abundance of universal love circulating in our own lives. This higher and beneficial energy field acts as an attractor pattern, driving away all remnants of fear. Instead of allowing illusions and inaccurate perceptions of our past to govern us, we can truly overcome fear with love.

Each one of us is charged with acting as an attractor pattern, creating an energy field of love and joy. It is our mission to shift the consciousness of our current reality from one where we are brainwashed to fear almost everything, to one where we are fearless and drawn to the Light.

The thorns of the "wag-'n-bietjie bos" can't get a good grip if you don't move too fast. When we take time to smell the roses—to enjoy what has been given to us from the beginning and not run after what society dictates—we come closer to our natural state: perfect peace. The radiance of Creation all around us then shines forth in all its beauty, rendering the thorns of fear unable to hook us. This practice does not depend on what we have or do; it arises simply out of who we are.

After five days in the bush at Umfolozi, with no soap or shampoo, dirty and tired, it was only the essence of each one of us that shone through. The rest was really immaterial.

Ultimately, it all comes down to the teaching of the Cherokee Indian grandfather. "There is a fight going on inside each of us", he told his grandchildren. "It is a terrible fight between two wolves. One wolf is evil—he is anger, fear, envy, sorrow, regret, greed, arrogance, self-pity, false pride, and ego. The other is good: joy, peace, love, serenity, humility, kindness, benevolence, generosity, compassion, and honesty. This same fight is going on inside of you and inside every other person, too." A little girl asked her granddad, "Which wolf will win?" The old Cherokee smiled and replied: "The one you feed".

We refrain from feeding the wolf of misery by not taking our marching orders from residual fear left over from our past. I recall being brought up to *fear* God; I wonder now if *respect* would not be a better word. Certainly, in my mission to educate young people, I have found that the most effective strategy is to teach them to respect themselves and everyone they meet. I also often tell my students, "Please take charge of your life!" I repeat the quote, "You are the master of your own destiny": in other words, your happiness is largely dependent on the way you view yourself and the world around you.

Life Skills Packet

I gave my students the following list of ten common counterproductive habits. They were asked to discuss each in the context of their own experience.

1. Procrastination
2. Indifference
3. Gossip
4. Pessimism
5. Indecision
6. Criticism
7. Complaining
8. Overcautious
9. Worry

10.Greed

I asked the students to choose the habit they felt most identified with, and to imagine what their future might look like without this habit. I invite you to do the same.

Ten Sticks

I opened this chapter with Thich Nhat Hahn's invitation to happiness. In the same spirit, I would like to offer you the following "ten sticks": kindling you can use to fuel the fire of happiness. These are drawn from a lovely little book called *Wokini* by Billy Mills, a Native American who won a gold medal in the 1960 Tokyo Olympics at the age of nineteen.

1. Realise I am the most special thing ever created.
2. Appreciate what life has given me.
3. View your life with optimism and hope for the future.
4. Set new and interesting goals.
5. Live each day as if it were your last.
6. Adjust to life accordingly.
7. Learn to live with and love yourself.
8. Never be a perfectionist.
9. Learn to laugh at life.
10.Learn to see the other's point of view.

Another list I have personally found very useful, from the same book, is the "eight lies of Iktumi", the spider and trickster. (I must say that my students don't seem to believe number 3!)

1. If only I were rich, then I'd be happy.
2. If only I were famous, then I'd be happy.
3. If only I could find the right person to marry, then I'd be happy.
4. If only I had more friends, then I'd be happy.

5. If only I were more attractive, then I'd be happy.

6. If only I weren't physically handicapped in any way, then I'd be happy.

7. If only someone close to me hadn't died, then I'd be happy.

8. If only the world were a better place, then I'd be happy.

Conclusion on Fear

Thich Nhat Hahn, as mentioned, says that there can be no happiness if fear is still present in us. But he also says that "without freedom, there is no happiness". Buddhists believe that we can cultivate freedom by the practice of *letting go.* This is associated with the Buddhist practice of *non-attachment.* When we loosen our grip on the fears of the past; when we relinquish our insistence on a desired outcome or personal opinion; only then can we truly practice *letting go.*

Practitioners of the ancient Chinese Taoist tradition describe this freedom in terms of *Wu Wei*—literally, "non-doing". The term means that we accept the moment spontaneously as it arises. We do not fight it, we do not resist it; that is just how it is. This means letting go of all attachment to certain outcomes—not so easy in our driven society! Wu Wei coincides with the notion of surrender in the face of fear, as illustrated in Dr David Hawkins's rattlesnake story. I have certainly not managed this feat yet!

When you stop to think about it, are any of the deadlines we're so attached to really that important? As Krishnamurti, the great Indian sage, revealed, "This is my secret: I don't mind what happens". Surely we would have fewer frustrations if we could subscribe to this wise philosophy. Not an easy practice, but definitely worth trying!

May you let go of all fear, all attachments, and all clinging to desired outcomes so you can truly experience happiness and be a beacon to others. By letting go and being an example of happiness yourself, you can inspire others to work on their own faults and so improve their own lives.

IDEAS:

____

____

____

____

ACTIONS:

____

____

____

____

Chapter 5
Taming the Mind—
Fact or Fiction?

So many self-help books nowadays tell us that the mind is a magnificent tool. I agree with that—but I would like to propose that our minds can be used for more than just accomplishments and the pursuit of happiness. And what is more, to achieve the highest purpose, we actually have to *lose* our minds.

Many of us are familiar with the writings of Rhonda Byrne. To date, she has written three books in the same vein: *The Secret*, *The Power,* and *The Magic*. Byrne says her intention is to bring "joy to billions". We could summarise her "secret" by saying that one must control one's thoughts and only think and speak of the good things that we want in life.

When it comes to the pursuit of happiness, imagination and good feelings definitely play a primary role. J.K. Rowling, creator of the *Harry Potter* books, said something similar in her graduation ceremony speech at Harvard University in 2008. She stressed that we don't need magic; we just need a powerful imagination to change the world for the better.

According to Rhonda Byrne, we can use the mind to help us give love—and love has no limits. The force of love can give us health, happiness, and an incredible zest for life. So I conclude that the primary purpose of the mind is, by love, to attract all good things into our lives.

The second purpose of love is to give the mind wings. Mind is the origin of imagination, which helps us to cross new rivers and come up with fresh ideas to improve our lives on Earth. We often fall into the habit of blaming a situation or the people supposedly responsible for our problems; but it is always better to look for a way to fix them. To state this differently: an optimistic mind supports the solution, rather than attacking the apparent causes of the problem. An optimistic mind makes it easier to cross new rivers.

However, we are also here to use the mind for grand intellectual pursuits. One of the most superb engineering achievements of the last century was the launching of Voyagers 1 and 2. Miraculously, these spacecraft are still out there in the cosmos—Voyager 1, apparently, now nineteen billion kilometres from Earth, having passed Neptune and Pluto. It is approaching the outer edge of our solar system as I write this. It takes tremendous intellectual genius to drive such technology.

Through the ages, humankind has also used the mind for prayer and devotion to a higher power. Our planet is peppered with evidence of ritual worship. The ancient site of Avebury in Wiltshire, England, is a remnant of Neolithic times, and England's largest henge monument. It consists of an outer circle of stones with two inner circles. Originally, there were apparently four hundred stones; now only twenty-seven are left.

Some of the Avebury stones are massive. The heaviest is the Swindon Stone, at sixty-five tons. There are also two closely placed stones that may have been the entrance to a ceremonial area. When I visited in 2012, the guide explained that, in general, these stones were used as a portal to other dimensions.

It's believed that worshippers gathered at Avebury to celebrate life and death. (The nearby Stonehenge site was used for worship of the sun and moon.) The site has a magical aura. The atmosphere of greatness and reverence, so rare in our contemporary world, makes one think that modern society might have lost something precious over the years.

During a trip to South Africa's Drakensberg Mountains, I came across a strange story about stones and extra-terrestrial contact. Your mind's imaginative powers will be challenged by this one! Apparently, there is a small beacon of stones on the top of Champagne Castle Peak, the second-highest peak in the Drakensberg at 3 377 metres. In 1990 an 82-year-old lady, Elizabeth Klarer, asked that a helicopter take her up to visit the beacon. Her belief was that spaceships used this beacon—and another three in Germany, Scotland and South America, respectively—to navigate celestial dimensions!

On arrival, Ms Klarer walked to the cairn of stones and proceeded to repack them. Then she pointed her marble-sized ring, made of crystal, at the cairn. To everyone's astonishment, the ring started to vibrate. For her, this was proof that the beacon was operating. If you visit the summit today, you will find a patch of ground where no grass grows. In the centre of a four-metre diameter area sits a small pile of stones. Ms Klarer told her guide that in the event of an alien invasion of Earth, this site and its three sister sites would be the safest places on the planet, as aliens would never destroy their own navigation system!

In sum, we can use our minds to attract 'good things"; to exercise our imagination; to think intellectually; and to pursue devotional ends. In order to attract good things, however, we first need to tame the mind. An untamed mind can actually attract bad things! In his DVD *Time Is an Illusion,* Eckhart Tolle points out that modern anxiety comes from our minds. We project ourselves into the future, where we build the most awful "what if" scenarios. Echoing some of India's enlightened masters, Tolle goes on to caution us against identifying with our thoughts. His advice is not to interpret, but just to be. To this famous spiritual teacher, the anxiety-driven modern person is actually mentally unsound!

Here, the mind represents an obstacle, rather than a resource. It leads us out of the moment, making it impossible to experience the beauty of the Now. Furthermore, if we believe our mind-made calamities, we will actually attract them. No wonder some ancient texts say that the mind is an enemy to those who can't control it! It is my opinion that this last area of the mind is the one that few people actually contemplate or endeavour to master.

"Taming the mind", as I understand it, means "to transcend the mind". Dr David Hawkins says that the mind is not really *you*; as soon as you have realised that, you are on your way to real freedom! Dr Hawkins says the spiritual seeker should specifically meditate to transcend the mind—its mental activities and limited perceptions. According to him, we will only realise the wonder of divinity and of all life if we can lose the ego.

The ego, in this sense, is everything that makes us who we are and that we cling to in order to survive. Dr Hawkins says that the ego and the mind are one and the same; thus, the mind actually blocks self-realisation. When we are "in the ego" we will always stay in duality: that is, we will think in terms of object and subject. Reality, from Dr Hawkins's perspective, is the Self, which is one. By contrast, subject and object assume the existence of two realities.

Ramana Maharshi is much more blunt in his explanation of our situation: "Everyone is committing suicide. The eternal blissful natural State has been smothered by this ignorant life."

Transcending the mind and conceiving a higher purpose seems to be very challenging! Everything we have learned and worked for—our image, money, job titles, status, and so forth—must be thrown out the window. Now, how many people are going to do that? My common sense says very few! So is the idea of taming the mind fact or fiction? Is it an achievable aim, or just a spiritual ideal destined to remain eternally inaccessible?

I might read that Indian spiritual guru Ramana Maharshi gained enlightenment at eighteen, but this information does not help me to tame my mind. The paradoxical state in which the mind is transcended looks to me like the product of a lifelong endeavour; nevertheless, it's a healthy carrot to hold out to those of us who are weary of modern life. Maybe our spiritual practices could lead us to real freedom. Perhaps a few of us could, after all, slip through the eye of that needle.

It seems that what it takes is surrender: surrender of the mind and all our false beliefs, so that we can open up to the blissful state of Spirit. This state, which we could call Enlightenment, can be described briefly as an unusual state of awareness that replaces our ordinary consciousness. I think of those massive stones at Avebury, and wonder whether approaching this "eternal blissful natural State" is the portal to a life experienced in all its beauty and fullness.

Life Skills Packet

My students are still establishing themselves on their respective life paths. To help them do that, we spend a whole lesson on the power of visualisation. I show them a short video based on the life and times of Magic Johnson, one of the USA's all-time great basketball players. Magic played for my university, Michigan State, when I studied there in 1980/81. He left in 1981 to join a team in Los Angeles, where his million-dollar contract was at that time the biggest ever in basketball.

So what is "visualisation"? It is a time-tested technique that a number of ancient spiritual traditions use to embody our own enlightened potential in the form of various imagined deities. In a more contemporary context, many athletes employ visualisation techniques to help them perform at their best. They visualise their performance beforehand, seeing themselves actually winning the race or game. So the athlete mentally creates a victorious outcome in her own mind before it really happens. This is a great example of how the mind can be used as a positive tool.

I can verify the power of this technique from my own athletic experience. There are two changeovers in triathlon: out of your wetsuit and on to your bike, and then from the bike into running shoes. At the world championships in Lausanne, our changeover times were clocked—it's that Swiss timing precision! My changeovers were about twenty seconds faster than anybody else's in my age group. In addition to practising them, I had visualised myself making speedy changeovers many times before the race.

Using the Mind for Visualisation

I also give my students an article by Vuyokazi Mnyengeza called "Pockets of Wealth". This article quotes Nigerian cement tycoon Aliko Dangote—at a personal worth of $16,1 billion, the richest man in Africa—from an interview with *Vanguard News.* "You must have not just a vision, but a plan that will help you realise it. Our vision in the next five years is to be a company that has $75 billion in market capitalisation, while being number one in Africa and one of the first one hundred in the world."

Then I ask my students to visualise their next day. Since choosing your day is such a fundamental skill, I have them do a visualisation exercise that originated with Dr Wayne Dyer. It seems to have worked for Elizabeth Gilbert, author of the bestselling *Eat, Pray, Love*, for she mentioned it during an interview with Oprah Winfrey.

Natalia Baker is another fan of this technique. The following version is from her book, *Seize the Day: A Guidebook for Changing Times.* The students are given an extract from the chapter called "Choice".

Choosing the Day You Want

I write down *what I really, really, really, really choose to manifest today* (if I don't have time to write it, I speak it aloud in the car or as I walk around). Choose what you are going to do: for instance, be at work, attend a meeting, lunch with a friend, sort some papers, buy a present, study, exercise. Notice that these activities are what you had scheduled anyway. Choose how you would like them to be and how *you* will be in the day and in these particular events.

An example: if you have invited some people to supper, you might write, I really, really, really, really choose to manifest deep meaningful sharing, fun and laughter, love and intimacy, a delicious meal, and an evening in which everyone thoroughly enjoys themself. I choose to be completely relaxed, loving, and at ease.

This is not only a training in choosing, but also in becoming a manifestor of the reality you desire. It gives you the sense of being in charge of your life. It is said that once you have made these conscious choices, your Higher Self assists you in fulfilling them.

Ten Essential Virtues[3]

In one of the Life Skills lessons, I ask students to match ten virtues with their correct descriptions. They are also instructed to give themselves a score from 0 to 10, indicating how they assess themselves in practising each virtue. Finally, students list the three virtues they particularly want to work on over the following six months.

1. Politeness

To be decent. First, we must acquire "the appearance and manner of good". This comes down to being well brought up: saying *please*, *thank you,* and *excuse me*.

2. Courage

Taking risks. This is the virtue of heroes, and probably the most universally admired. It is a form of excellence—the opposite of cowardice, but also of laziness and spinelessness. To confront; to master and overcome fear.

---

[3] From the book *A Short Treatise on the Great Virtues the Uses of Philosophy in Everyday Life*, by André Comte-Sponville, originally published in French (1996).

3. Temperance

Students often have difficulty defining this one, but it is such
a worthwhile virtue! Moderation makes us masters of our
pleasure instead of its slaves. It prefers quality to quantity,
and ultimately yields greater enjoyment than excess can.

4. Simplicity

Openness of gaze; purity of heart; sincerity of speech. This is
the spiritual virtue of being in the present, which brings joy,
lightness, and tranquillity. It is the opposite of duplicity,
complexity, and pretension. Thus, it is the virtue of the wise
and the wisdom of the saints!

5. Humour

Taking yourself lightly; freeing the self from ego fixation;
transmuting sadness into joy by being able to laugh at
yourself. Always love smilingly.

6. Purity

Love unmixed with self-interest: clean, spotless, and unsoiled.
This love gives and protects; its desire is non-offensive and
non-violent. A virtue that elevates and celebrates.

7. Gentleness

Courage without violence; strength without harshness; love
without demand. A strength that lies somewhere between
compassion and generosity, refusing to do harm.

8. Generosity

It is almost impossible to love without giving—of self, of time,
of money … In giving, we realise our own freedom and feel
confident to use it, so, giving naturally leads to self-esteem.
This virtue is the opposite of selfishness, and thus leads to

freedom from the ego self. Thus, it is said to cultivate greatness of spirit.[4]

9. Compassion

Literally, to feel with another, particularly when that other is suffering. It is the opposite of coldness, indifference, and insensitivity. Ultimately, this virtue describes the ability to empathise with all living beings that suffer.

10. Gratitude

To thank is to give; to be gracious means to share. Our appreciation gives back a little of the joy that we have received or experienced. How could we *not* be thankful to the sun for existing? For life, or flowers, or birds? When we contemplate that without the rest of the universe we would not exist, we give birth to universal appreciation.

Curiosita and Self-Assessment

I tell my students that Leonardo Da Vinci's first principle for living fully was *curiosita*: an insatiable curiosity about life and an unrelenting quest for continuous learning.

Then students complete a self-assessment form:[5]

- ❖ I keep a journal or notebook to record my insights and questions
- ❖ I take adequate time for contemplation and reflection
- ❖ I am always learning something new
- ❖ When I am faced with an important decision, I actively seek out different perspectives
- ❖ I am a voracious reader

---

[4] A wonderful habit to cultivate is tithing: contributing 10 per cent of your income to charity, social upliftment, or some other worthy cause.

[5] Borrowed from the training department of South Africa's Standard Bank.

- ❖ I learn from little children

- ❖ I am skilled at identifying and solving problems

- ❖ My friends would describe me as open-minded and curious

- ❖ When I hear or read a new word or phrase, I look it up and make a note of it

- ❖ I know a lot about other cultures and am always learning more

- ❖ I know or am involved in learning a language other than my native one

- ❖ I solicit feedback from my friends, relations, and colleagues

- ❖ I love learning

Next, students read the ten "power questions" below and choose one they particularly like:

1. When am I most naturally myself? What people, places and activities allow me to feel most fully myself?

2. What is the one thing I could stop doing, or start doing, or do differently, *starting today,* that would most improve the quality of my life?

3. What is my greatest talent?

4. How can I get paid for doing what I love?

5. Who are my most inspiring role models?

6. How can I best be of service to others?

7. What is my heart's deepest desire?

8. How I am perceived by my closest friend? My worst enemy? My boss, my children, my co-workers, etc.?

9. What are the blessings of my life?

10. What legacy would I like to leave?

Then students do the following contemplation exercise:

Take one of the above ten "power questions" and write it in large letters on a blank sheet of paper. Then hold the question in your mind for the next ten minutes.

- ❖ Sit in a quiet place and keep the question in front of you.

- ❖ Relax and breathe deeply, allowing extended exhalations.

- ❖ When your mind starts to wander, bring it back by reading the question again, out loud.

It is particularly valuable to do this contemplation exercise before going to sleep, and again upon waking. You will find that if you practise it sincerely, your mind will "incubate" insights overnight.

All of these exercises are intended to help students achieve happiness. When we are happy, we are in tune with Spirit. Whether we will ever reach the real eternal blissful State, of course, is all a matter of grace. However, the Buddha—who really knew how to control the mind—said: "Thoughts well guarded bring happiness".

Study Methods and Time Management

Since the programme was developed for young students, we do discuss study methods as well as time management—all things that are governed by the mind.

Students are urged to study cyclically—in other words, to study to the end of a certain chapter or a certain page rather than being guided by linear time. So say they are going to a party at 9 PM. They should set their target from their study material—for instance, study until the end of Chapter Two and stop at that point. They should not sit and study till 8.30 PM; this is not conducive to optimal learning.

I demonstrated to these students the "Big Rocks" exercise of Stephen Covey. Covey describes the visit of a time-management expert to a group of business students. To drive home a point, this expert used an illustration I'm sure those students will never forget. After I share it with you, you'll never forget it either.

"Okay," the expert told these high-powered over-achievers, "time for a quiz." He set a one-gallon, wide-mouthed Mason jar on a table in front of him. Then he produced about a dozen fist-sized rocks and carefully placed them, one at a time, into the jar.

When the jar was filled to the top and no more rocks would fit inside, he asked, "Is this jar full?" Everyone in the class said, "Yes." Then he said, "Really?" He reached under the table and pulled out a bucket of gravel. Then he dumped some gravel in and shook the jar, causing pieces of gravel to work themselves down into the spaces between the big rocks.

Then he smiled and asked the group once more, "Is the jar full?" By this time the class was on to him. "Probably not", one of them answered. "Good!" he replied. And he reached under the table and brought out a bucket of sand. He started dumping the sand in and it went into all the spaces left between the rocks and the gravel. Once more he asked the question, "Is this jar full?"

"No!" the class shouted. Once again he said, "Good!" Then he grabbed a pitcher of water and began to pour it in until the jar was filled to the brim. Then he looked up at the class and asked, "What is the point of this illustration?"

One eager beaver raised his hand and said, "The point is, no matter how full your schedule is, if you try really hard, you can always fit some more things into it!"

"No", the speaker replied, "that's not the point. The truth this illustration teaches us is: if you don't put the big rocks in first, you'll never get them in at all."

What are the big rocks in your life? A project that you want to accomplish? Time with your loved ones? Your faith, your education, your finances? A cause? Teaching or mentoring others? Remember to put these "big rocks" in first or you'll never get them in at all.

I also aim to teach my students to have a bit of order in the planning of their day. Some people make lists; others prefer to work with an image or map. Whatever strategy works for them, they should apply. I point out that certain daily tasks simply have to be done. When we bring these into consciousness and set priorities, we wind up having more free time to do the things we value and enjoy.

I also give students Covey's two-by-two time management matrix. It looks like this:

	URGENT	**NOT URGENT**
IMPORTANT	Deadlines Crises Last-minute preparations	Relationship building Personal development Employee training Exercise
NOT IMPORTANT	Some emails & calls Many interruptions	Facebook Excessive TV Time wasters

Students fill in their own items in each box. The ideal, of course, is to function mostly in the important/not urgent quadrant.

IDEAS:

ACTIONS:

Chapter 6
A Mirror for the Soul

*There is something about the outside of a horse
that is good for the inside of a man.*

—Winston Churchill

Mr Churchill was so right! I have had many profound experiences with horses. One of the most amazing and unforgettable was a trip I took along South Africa's southern Wild Coast with a Welsh friend.

We flew from Cape Town to the small coastal city of East London and spent our first two days at the Endalweni Private Game Reserve. There we rode for about three hours every day, watching game. This helped to get our riding muscles in shape for the epic twenty-seven kilometre trip across the pont over the Kei River. (The pont—really a barge—is a large wooden structure that takes cars, horses etc. across the river.)

My friend was not an experienced rider. Fortunately, she was allotted a wonderful 18-year-old mare, Starlight. On beach canters and over rough terrain like rivers and steep banks, this mare pretty much did her own thing. My friend kept her cool admirably and survived all the ups and downs with great success. She managed to stay on Starlight without falling off once!

I am an experienced rider with a jumping background, so I was given a super-fast gelding called Asante. This beautiful white horse was an ideal mount for me. He and I had some awesome, thrilling canters on the long stretches of white beach we traversed on our journey.

We spent one night at the lovely Wavecrest Hotel before saddling up our mounts again. A strong wind was whipping up sandstorms on the beaches, so on our way back to the Kei River we had to head inland, making the return trip a few kilometres longer. This new route involved some arduous climbs and downhills on very rough terrain.

When we finally arrived back at Morgan Bay after this long and taxing trip, I raised a glass of champagne to my Welsh friend's courage, the expertise of our two horses, and our excellent guides.

The Magic of Horses

In June 2012, I took a sabbatical from my university lectureship in Cape Town and headed for England. There, I saw the amazing movie *Buck*. This 2011 documentary follows the life of Buck Brannaman, a 49-year-old American cowboy who was a technical advisor for Robert Redford's 1998 blockbuster *The Horse Whisperer*. *Buck* won the audience award at the Sundance Film Festival. The *Los Angeles Times* called the movie "extraordinary ... an exceptional slice of Americana about the kind of unsung hero that America loves to love".

I liked the "unsung hero" aspect, but what really spoke to me was how Buck worked with the healing power of horses. I felt a thrill of recognition when he said, "Your horse is a mirror of your soul. Sometimes you would not like what you see. Sometimes you will." A 2013 article on the healing power of horses in *Kindred Spirit*, the UK's leading spiritual magazine, echoed Buck Brannaman's approach: the horse mirrors the owner's feelings, so anyone wanting to master a horse should first master her- or himself.

As a behavioural kinesiologist, I help clients on their journeys of self-discovery. So I found especially compelling those scenes where Buck told the owner of a misbehaving animal, "This horse tells me quite a lot about you"—a remark that would often reduce the owner to tears. Little wonder, then, that Buck says, "I am helping horses with people problems"!

Another uplifting aspect of the movie was to see what a wonderful and peaceful man Buck has become, despite childhood abuse by a very angry and violent father. It seems that horses were an important part of his own healing path.

Horses are such beautiful and intelligent beings! When I was a young rider in the modern pentathlon event for South Africa in the 1980s, they taught me some exceptional lessons.

One of many such lessons came while I was training at the United States Olympic Centre for Modern Pentathlon in San Antonio, Texas. One morning I was given Flash Cadillac, a lovely chestnut horse with a flowing white mane. Flash Cadillac was very energetic—he just wanted to canter, and kept trying to run away with me. "This horse doesn't want to listen!" I thought. So I took him into a nearby paddock and tried to ride him to exhaustion. I think Flash Cadillac must have been laughing at my vain attempts to control him. For about half an hour we cantered, first to the left, then to the right—but of course, the horse was much stronger than I was. The next morning I was stiff as a rod. I literally had to roll my body out of bed for my running session!

In our high-tech world, we have become used to controlling things instantly with the flip of a switch. But it takes time, patience, and attention to make a relationship with an animal. Learning how to ride a horse can teach us—and especially children—invaluable lessons about relationships. Trying to dominate the horse simply doesn't work, as Flash Cadillac taught me, and as Buck Brannaman kept having to tell his clients. The only way to get a horse to do what you want is to work *with* it, rather than getting into a power struggle.

Our intimate human relationships often reveal the dangers of our compulsion to control. I'm reminded, again, of my experience sitting at the feet of the remarkable Zen monk Thich Nhat Hahn at his Plum Village retreat centre in Bordeaux. This spiritual master points out that love is a *process,* rather than a destination. So we derive more benefit from working to understand the other than by trying to exert control. It was only in my forties, after some workshops at the Breakthru Institute, that I was eventually able to relinquish my own controlling behaviour.

To really understand another person, we have to establish genuine communication. The bond between horse and human demonstrates a long and moving history of just such communication. Buck puts it beautifully: "Everything you do with a horse is a dance". Our centuries-old dance with horses is a genuine and rich treasure, always available for our enjoyment and upliftment.

In Tune with All Animals

I feel there is an urgent need for humanity to recognise our common cause with all living things. So I had my life skills students watch *The Animal Communicator*. This South African-made documentary features Cape Town local Anna Breytenbach (daughter of well-known photographer Cloete Breytenbach). Anna's particular gift enables her to communicate with animals. Some amazing footage demonstrated just how thoroughly she was in tune with animals!

A story that particularly impressed me was that of a beautiful black panther owned by ex-policeman Jurg Ohlsson and his wife, Katrin. Jurg could do nothing with this awesome big cat, which he had named Diablo. The animal merely snarled at him and refused to emerge from his night shelter. Mr Ohlsson was sceptical that an animal communicator could help, but he was persuaded to give it a try.

Anna went straight to the panther's enclosure and began immediately to communicate with him. The panther expressed concern about two leopard cubs, his neighbours at the time he was removed from his previous home in a European zoo. What had happened to them? Then he told Anna that he did not want to be called Diablo, a name associated with the dark and devilish. He wanted to be renamed.

These revelations took the Ohlssons totally by surprise. They told Anna the leopard cubs were fine; they were actually in their care as well. Taking note of the panther's request for a different name, they decided on Spirit. That afternoon, for the first time in six months, the panther came out of his den and seemed restful and at peace. The reaction of his carer, the policeman, was heartrending. Jury wept, insisting that he had never believed such a thing was possible.

Not only did Anna change the life of this beautiful black cat; the Ohlssons have now taken her course in animal communication, and revel in their newly acquired skills. Being in tune with animals creates feelings of happiness and delight. What a lovely gift!

I felt it important that my students understand our responsibility to cultivate the life skills necessary to save our planet from the forces of greed, aggression, and ignorance. I believe that the urge to control stems largely from fears about the future. May the new millennium bring the human race back to the *now*—just the same way as when we are riding a trail, completely in tune with the magnificent animal beneath the saddle. Once one can trust the unknown, whether in the form of a horse, another human being, or life itself, one can relax and just be.

IDEAS:

ACTIONS:

Chapter 7
The Need for Exercise on Our Quest

I'm sure that every single soul on earth wants to have lots and lots of energy! An abundance of life force makes us stand out in a crowd—everyone can see we have something special. But how do we cultivate this unseen thing, this golden stream that chi kung masters call *chi*? Chi Kung (sometimes spelled *qigong*) is an ancient Chinese exercise system that works with the flows of energy in both body and mind. Our chi is influenced by what we eat and drink, of course; it also increases when we spend more time in nature. But to really increase our life force, we need to cultivate stamina and flexibility, as well.

In my job as a university lecturer, I was moved to a new campus. The adjustment and getting used to the unfamiliar surroundings took their toll: I left work tired and grumpy. No matter how hard I tried to fit in a late afternoon yoga class, I just didn't want to spend any time in another building. Yoga is a great gift to our bodies, and at other times I've found it wonderfully energising. But in this situation I had a yearning to be outside in nature. So I drove up to the Kirstenbosch Botanic Gardens and went for a run in Cecilia Forest. The trees, fresh air, and wind supplied me with new vigour, and I felt topped up again. I lost that bad mood and returned home in good spirits.

Mindfulness is another energising factor. Do we stay with what is put in front of us? Do we really live only in this moment? A busy mind can be very tiring; it takes us out of what is happening now. It is also based on untruths: our thoughts are mostly illusionary, because they're filtered through our own way of seeing things.

One Zen master challenged his pupils to walk on a busy street. As they did so, he instructed them to focus their attention on the energy centre a little below the navel known in Chinese anatomy as the lower *tantien*. This helped them stay focused and aware that they were walking. As a result, all the people moving in their direction intuitively—unconsciously—felt their focus and got out of the way! So a focused student discovered that he or she created an open channel to walk through a crowd.

This story brings to mind the old Bible story of Moses parting the waters of the Red Sea so his people could walk through safely. When we are focused and mindful, we are also more in harmony with all that is. We are more in union with ourselves—rather than split into two, with mind thinking and body on automatic pilot.

I am an avid follower of chi kung. I cannot speak too highly of this exquisite art of being. It is a way of life that encourages me to be in tune with my body, breath, and mind. Not surprisingly, chi kung brings tremendous health benefits—improving digestion, promoting circulation, and preventing illnesses, to name but a few.

During the Chinese Cultural Revolution in 1966–76, numerous chi kung practitioners were thrown in jail. The practice was actually illegal in China until the early 1980s. As recently as September 1999, the Chinese health ministry issued laws restricting all forms of chi kung. Why? Because chi kung promotes independent thinking! In the new world we are creating now, may independent thinking be welcomed and embraced.

Go to Nature

Most traditional Eastern ways of cultivating energy mimic the movements of animals. I experienced some of these movements personally when I attended a chi kung course with the Swiss master Max Weier. He taught us a series of movements called "The Five Manchurians". Here, each movement is centred on one of the five main organs of the body—lungs, kidneys, liver, heart, and stomach—with the purpose of stimulating and energising that organ.

Traditionally, one starts with the lungs. For these we practised "white crane ascending into the heavens", a beautiful flowing movement that looks like a bird ascending into the sky.

According to Chinese belief, our sexual energy resides in our kidneys. The movement that stimulates this pair of organs is called "sitting on tiger".

Third is the liver, the organ most susceptible to climate changes and to travelling. Any change of environment can throw the liver out of balance—especially, of course, if we drink too much! The liver exercise is called "lazy cat stretching".

The movement that stimulates the fourth main organ, the heart, reminds me of the characters riding flying dragons in the epic movie *Avatar*. It had the apt name of "riding the sky horse".

The final movement, associated with the stomach, is "golden rooster stands proudly on one leg". This one became my favourite because it flows so naturally. I also like the way it borrows from the Eastern martial arts styles.

Many contemporary magazines, especially *Men's Health*, avidly promote the so-called "six-pack" look. Funnily enough, Max told us, the Eastern energy system doesn't advocate a six-pack at all. Enlarged muscles around the abdominal area apparently confuse our main energy centre, the lower tantien. So we actually have less energy when we carry a six-pack!

Max also spoke out against the current tendency of young people to wear jeans that sit far below the hips, since this exposes their kidneys to the cold. If our kidneys are the source of our sexual energy, we should try to keep them warm and protected at all times. Max himself wears a magnetic belt in the winter to keep his kidneys warm and functioning well. Chi kung masters believe that, as our biggest energy receptacle, these organs should be well looked after!

As a behavioural kinesiologist, I found the emotional aspects of the five organs particularly interesting. Here's a quick summary.

Lungs: To relax the lungs is to feed your courage. The negative aspect is grief, which is stored in the lungs and will negatively influence them. The healing colour to visualise is white.

Kidneys: The positive aspect of the kidneys is lots of vitality. The negative aspect is fear; people who are fearful tend to have weak kidneys. The colour associated with the kidneys is blue.

Liver: The liver is known as the anger centre of the body, and anger is its negative aspect. The positive aspect of the liver is generosity. Green is the colour to visualise here.

Heart: The positive aspect of the heart is laughter and joy; the negative aspects are cruelty (a closed heart) and nervousness. The associated colour is, not surprisingly, red.

Stomach: The positive aspect of the stomach is trust, while the negative aspect is worry. The colour is yellow.

You'll get the most benefit out of chi kung movements in the early morning, when the chi in the air is at its most potent.

Sounds also influence our chi. On my new campus, the building where I work is under construction. The constant noise is nerve-wracking and draining, especially while I'm lecturing. By the same token, certain sounds will energise and relax specific organs. These so-called "healing sounds" can be quite advantageous for our general health, and some of them are incorporated into chi kung postures and movements. But the best sound of all is silence! Sitting quietly in meditation, either at home or in nature, does wonders for our chi levels.

Life Skills Packet

As mentioned, I had my life skills students run a one-kilometre time trail. It is always very heart-warming for me when students come to love the movement and adhere to an exercise routine of their own accord. Some of them start going diligently to the gym, others start running regularly. Adhering to their exercise with discipline obviously brings benefits for their studies as well. I believe it also improves their self-esteem.

Not everyone loves exercise, but most health magazines assure us that it should be part of our daily routine. I would suggest doing some kind of exercise or stretching at least five times a week. We're told that we derive the greatest benefit from exercise routines that last longer than thirty minutes. Based on my own athletic experience, I'd like to add that at least one exercise bout per week should push your heart rate up above 140 beats per minute. In a fit and young person, the heart rate will come down within a minute after that bout to 120, which is known as "the pulse plateau".

I once watched a YouTube video featuring the 90th birthday party of Jean Veloz. This former Hollywood actress still dances like a 20-year-old—maybe even better and more energetically! She is obviously is still living her passion for dance—to jive and rock and roll! May you, like this remarkable woman, make the best lifestyle choices for yourself, so that you have more than enough chi to enjoy the miracle of life.

IDEAS:

ACTIONS:

Chapter 8
Eating Healthily—
Do Our Bodies Have the Wisdom to Eat Right?

Nutrition is such a contentious issue. However, it is also very important: all humans want health, wealth, and happiness—and much of that depends on what we put into our bodies.

In my behavioural kinesiology practice I have worked with over three hundred clients. Based largely on this body of experience, I take the liberty of offering my opinions on this crucial issue.

Giving Our Bodies the Nutrition They Need

Many teachers, metaphysical and otherwise, have spoken of the innate wisdom of the body. One of these is Cape Town's Natalia Baker. She maintains that the body is much wiser than the mind, for our minds have been programmed and thus cannot perceive the truth. Following this logic, we should strive to be in tune with our bodies, so as to make use of this essential tool. Then we would be able to read the truth intuitively.

To be in tune with one's body, one must feed it the right nutrients. But what are those? It seems that virtually every week, nutritional scientists are changing their minds about what is good for us and what isn't.

A most revealing *Time* magazine article by Bryan Walsh declares that eating fat is good for the body. A healthy diet, from this point of view, includes butter, cream, and other fatty foods. This advice contradicts virtually all the previous literature on nutrition.

As it happens, the diet featured in *Time* is exactly what Dr Tim Noakes of Cape Town's Sport Science Institute has been advocating for years. He is South Africa's foremost proponent of the high-fat, low-carbohydrate Banting diet. The prominent South African health consumers' website *Health 24* posted the following "rules" for following the Banting diet:

1. Remember: this is not a high-protein diet. It's a high-fat, medium-protein, low-carbohydrate way of eating.

2. Choose real foods that look like what they are, and cook them from scratch.

3. Fat is not the enemy. Enjoy it!

4. Eat only when you are hungry. Eat until you are satisfied; then stop.

5. Don't eat when you are not hungry. Occasionally skipping a meal when you don't feel like eating won't kill you.

6. Stop snacking. You don't need to—it's just a habit.

7. Avoid sugar. It's an addiction, and to kick it, it's probably best to go cold turkey. But if you need to make a transition, substitute with stevia, xylitol or erythritol—not artificial sweeteners.

8. No "grains" of any kind.

9. No (or very little) fruit. Think of it as a sweet rather than a health snack.

10. Embrace eggs. They're healthy, satisfying, and very good for you.

Dr Noakes's theories aren't the only authoritative nutritional guidelines available to us, of course. The American doctor T. Colin Campbell, along with some collaborators, authored a 2005 book called *The China Study*. This book reports on a nutritional study conducted in sixty-five rural Chinese counties. The authors came to the conclusion that "people who eat a whole-food, plant-based/vegan diet—avoiding all animal products, including beef, pork, poultry, fish, eggs, cheese and milk, and reducing their intake of processed food and refined carbohydrates—will escape, reduce or reverse the development of numerous diseases".

Nutritional Kinesiology

My own view of such contrasting findings agrees with that of Natalia Baker: we should really just listen to the body. What I mean by that is not just trying to figure out how we feel about various foods, but applying empirical testing by means of kinesiology.

Our muscles respond very directly to true and false statements, respectively. Try this with a friend: hold your arm out at right angles to your body, and have your friend press down on it while you say something you know to be true—perhaps "My name is _______". Then say something you know to be false, such as "My name is Richard Gere". Your friend will find it much easier to push your arm down when you say something untrue.

Using this natural response to what the body knows to be true, I typically perform a nutritional analysis for all my kinesiology clients. I test their responses to grains; dairy; meat; nuts, seeds, and oils; fruits; low-starch vegetables; high-starch vegetables; nightshades (a species of flowering plant that includes tomato, potato, peppers, and eggplant); beverages; and miscellaneous other foods, such as yeast, vinegar, tofu, and food colouring.

I have found that the most frequent culprits, in terms of taxing people's systems, are grains, meats, and dairy products. Occasionally, someone will test positively for nightshades (meaning that this person should not eat one or some of the foods under this heading), and also for certain kinds of nuts. I have also seen some clients who should not drink coffee or caffeinated teas, as well as some who are allergic to sugar.

With apologies to supporters of both Dr Noakes and Dr Campbell, my own conclusion is that we can happily eat seeds and oils, as well as all vegetables and fruit. Whether we can eat meat, dairy, grains, nightshades, or nuts will depend on our particular body's makeup.

What about Fruit?

Fruit and vegetables have been given to us from the earliest emergence of the human race. Personally, I cannot believe that they could be harmful to our bodies when eaten in moderation. A 2014 study of half a million people found, in fact, that eating fruit every day cuts the risk of cardiovascular disease by up to 40 percent.[6] That said, fruit does contain fructose—in other words, sugar. So unless you engage in physical training on a daily basis, it might be wise to count your calories or watch your carbohydrate intake.

Here are some fruits and their associated carbs and calories.[7]

Raw fruit (per 100 gm)	Carbs (grams)	Calories
Strawberries	8,7	37
Guavas	15,0	62
Watermelon	6,4	62
Pears	15,3	61
Pineapple	13,7	52
Apples	14,5	58

---

[6] The study was led by Dr Huaidong Du, from Oxford in the UK.

[7] Excerpted from "The Complete South African Kilojoule, Calorie and Carbohydrate Counter" in *Good Taste*, January 2015, p.59.

Bananas	33,3	127
Mangoes	16,8	66
Litchis	16,4	64
Nectarines	14,6	64
Grapes	17,3	67

A good habit to cultivate is to drink freshly pressed fruit and vegetable juice first thing in the morning, about twice a week. My own two favourites are beetroot juice (two beetroots, two pears, one cucumber, and a knob of fresh ginger) and apple/carrot juice (one apple, one pear, four celery sticks, four carrots, and a knob of fresh ginger).

I am in my sixties as I write this. Accordingly, I have come up with a list of foods I would call "must-eats" for everyone over the age of fifty. This list distils most of the nutritional studies I've looked at. Once we pass the age of fifty, it becomes especially important to support, rather than stress, our hard-working bodies.

1. Full cream, plain, unsweetened yoghurt
2. Oats
3. Salmon, pilchards, or sardines
4. Avocados
5. Beans and lentils.

Diets

I am not particularly in favour of dieting. I have been an athlete all my life and it was never necessary to diet. If you need to lose weight, I suggest you first test whether your body is okay with meats and dairy, and then follow either the Banting or, better still, the popular 5–2 diet. This latter is known as "the fasting diet", and involves calorie restriction for two non-consecutive days a week. The other five days, you can eat anything you like! A devout Muslim friend tells me that this is exactly what the Prophet Muhammad suggested more than a thousand years ago. As they say, there is nothing new under the sun!

It was heartening to note that the *Time* article cited above concludes with the observation that "how we eat ... matters as much as what we eat". To enjoy food with friends and family in a relaxed atmosphere might well mean more to our eventual health than what is on our plates!

Accordingly, I fully support the drinking of wine, which can greatly enhance the pleasure of being with friends and family. Most medical studies suggest that a daily glass of wine for women, and two for men, is good for our health. Red wine, in particular, is rich in resveratrol, which is said to reduce the bad cholesterol in our blood. Wine also has a healthy dose of anti-oxidants, which might protect the memory from age-related deterioration.

Patrick San Francesco, an enlightened being of Goa, India (see Chapter 9), proposes that there is no specifically "spiritual" diet. You can eat whatever you like; being spiritual doesn't necessarily mean you have to be a vegetarian! This accords with my own view that we should follow the innate wisdom of our bodies, and eat what is required for our respective unique setups.

It is true for virtually all of us, however, that our bodies tend towards problematic acidity. But our saliva is alkaline, so when we chew our food at least about thirty times, it arrives in our stomachs in much better shape for optimal digestion and absorption.

The Benefits of Higher Consciousness

As will have become evident in previous chapters, I am an admirer of Dr David Hawkins of the Spiritual Institute in

Sedona, Arizona. Dr Hawkins, bless his soul, died peacefully at home in September 2012. He maintained that attaining a higher consciousness, or spiritual maturity, grants immunity against the detrimental effects of unhealthy foods. In other words, the more loving, kind, and considerate we become, and the fewer negative feelings we cultivate, the healthier we are likely to be.

In my own kinesiology practice, I have come across clients who are very spiritually mature but who still suffer from allergies and other physical problems. I believe this is due to past lives. The notion of reincarnation is not unique to Eastern religions, incidentally—the 20th-century American Christian Edgar Cayce wrote prolifically about it.

Standing Together for Our Future

Elizabeth Gilbert, in her novel *The Signature of All Things,* makes a strong case for the evolutionary nature of our universe. From this perspective, only the strongest species survive. It makes sense to me that only the strongest and fittest among us—physically, mentally, emotionally, and spiritually—will eventually make it through the massive changes our planet is going through.

The founder of the Universal Sufi Movement, Hazrat Inayat Khan, predicted the future of the world back in the 1920s. Everything would eventually be harmonious, he told his followers; there will be great joy and peace on earth. People will tolerate each other's beliefs, rather than going to war over them.

This seems an unlikely prophecy at the moment, but by holding it in our collective consciousness; we might just be able to turn the status quo around. We are certainly at a crossroads. If we stand together, I believe that we can create a new civilisation in which all are free and in which social justice reins. Otherwise, we will continue to be divided and so probably see the end of life on this planet.

Reversing the destructive trajectory so many human beings are now caught up in may sound like an overwhelming task, but it begins with each one of us. We make our contribution by simply working hard to improve the lives and health of ourselves and our dependants. The choice is yours; you are the one steering the boat. The famous line by poet William Ernest Henley comes to mind: "I am the master of my fate; I am the captain of my soul". This remains true whether the seas are rough or calm. It's all part of the precious journey called *life*!

Life Skills Packet

Healthy eating was an important part of the life skills teachings. Most of my students, from what I could see during the days I spent around them, tank up on fizzy cool drinks, chips, and other cheap convenience foods.

One of the first things I do in the Life Skills course is to invite a student to help me demonstrate some simple kinetic testing. I easily push the student's arm down in the presence of white refined sugar. Then I replace the sugar with honey. The same student's arm remains strong. Next, I repeat the test with Coca Cola and beer. Believe it or not, the arm goes down with the Coke but stays strong with the beer!

Finally, I offer my students some tips from the book *The Okinawa Way*, a four-week health regime based on a study of unusually healthy and long-lived residents of Okinawa, in the East China Sea.

The Okinawa Way

In her book *Prime Time,* Jane Fonda proposes that life is not in the shape of a parabola, as is commonly thought. We don't go downhill after forty, she said; rather, life is a stairway going ever upwards. According to Ms Fonda, old age should be a joyous time of life, because we are more mature and sorted!

The inhabitants of Japan's Okinawa islands are a living testament to this approach. The islands boast a population of around 1.3 million—four hundred of whom are centenarians! Most of them are still active and healthy. Here exercise is a way of life: many older people practise martial arts and traditional dancing, as well as gardening and walking. They nurture their *chi* and live a balanced lifestyle that is in tune with nature's way. *Nuchi gusui*, the islanders like to say: "May your food (and lifestyle) heal".

The standard Okinawan diet features low-calorie, plant-based foods high in unrefined carbohydrates; lots of fruit, vegetables, and legumes (soya and other beans); and whole grains. Most people eat at least two servings of flavonoid-rich soy products daily, and fish rich in Omega-3 several times a week. Dairy products and meat are rarely eaten. They also subscribe to *hara hachi bu*: eating only until 80 per cent full.

Perhaps the dietary customs of Okinawa are what we have come to call "conscious eating". But whatever we call it, the Okinawans' relationship with food must certainly revitalise the experience of eating with the joy and pleasure we have lost in our jungle of rushed meals and convenience foods.

In addition to eating well, Okinawans live a deeply spiritual life, blending a Taoist reverence for nature with Confucian respect for others. Just like the inhabitants of Thich Nhat Hanh's Plum Village, they routinely take one day of the week off for relaxation and play. One 95-year-old Okinawan whose photo appears in the book is the picture of youth and vitality. Sporting a chic floral shirt, hip sunglasses, and a Panama hat, he looks footloose, fancy free, laid back, and colourful. This man was interviewed in his office; he still worked as a consultant!

One of my own heroes is John Dobson, who invented the Dobson telescope. He taught until well into his eighties, even then a picture of health and vitality. He showed many people all over the world how to construct a homemade Dobson telescope so that they could admire the heavens from their own homes. Dobson liked to say that "the exterior decorator (meaning the Divine) has done a beautiful job"!

Finally, my students receive the following information from a *National Geographic* article called "Shopping by the Numbers". It rates foods from 1 to 100, based on a general understanding of what promotes good health. The following list features all the foods that score higher than 80.

100 Broccoli

100 Blueberries

100 Orange

100 Green beans

99 Pineapple

99 Radish

98 Summer Squash

96 Apple

96 Green cabbage

96 Tomato

94 Clementine

94 Watermelon

93 Mango

91 Nonfat milk

91 Fresh figs

91 Grapes

91 Banana

89 Avocado

88 Oatmeal

83 Blackberries

82 Sockeye salmon

82 Raw almonds

82 Raw pecans

82 Arugula

82 Brown rice

82 Snapper

81 Milk (1% fat)

I am largely in accord with these ratings, except that I would rather drink full-cream milk. It contains only about 3,7 per cent fats, which themselves contain lots of vitamins.

However, as I tell my students, vitamins are not a panacea for good health. No study has ever found that it is beneficial to use vitamin supplementation. I suggest that they supplement their diets daily with two cold-pressed Omega fish oil tablets – Omega-3 fish oil.

How one eats and drinks, as the *Time* article points out, is probably more important than what one eats. My own philosophy is that one should enjoy life to the full—eat, drink, and be merry—as long as you can do it without harming your body.

IDEAS:

ACTIONS:

Chapter 9
Everything Is Possible

I always wondered what a man who channels divine energy would look like. In August 2014, I was privileged to attend a talk by such a healer: Patrick San Francesco of Goa, India. I also attended his workshop on healing the next day in Cape Town.

Patrick was down-to-earth, funny, and totally natural. He is tall and thin and speaks English very well, with a faint Indian accent. I heard from his attendants that he does not eat much—apparently, only once a week. He reportedly also sleeps just one hour each night. I guess the divine energy that he channels sustains him adequately.

For Patrick, it is imperative that we celebrate the wonder of life. He is of the opinion that when we interact socially with others, our happiness should overwhelm them.

When he was just about three years old, Patrick realised that if his dear mother fed him every day, how much more loving would be our Divine Mother/Father! During his talk, he told us that when he was seventeen a friend played a prank on him, stretching some fishing line across the top of a staircase to trip him up. Sure enough, Patrick fell down the stairs and damaged his neck. The family's doctor told his parents that their now-bedridden son would be a quadriplegic for the rest of his life. Patrick, already a healer since the age of four, told the physician very confidently that he would stand up in three days—and he did!

I didn't know what to expect from Patrick's colour healing workshop that weekend. It was frankly a bit way out for this scientist, but I trusted that he knew what he was doing. Patrick instructed us to visualise certain colours in meditation, and to build a protective egg around ourselves. One of the participants reported that after one such healing session, she had been able to move a frozen shoulder and arm for the first time in months!

According to Patrick, he sees twelve hundred patients a day! One of them, an American, offered a large donation to Patrick's charity (the Samarpan Foundation) for solving his problem. Every day, this man had suffered mysterious and debilitating pain in his right leg. No other doctor or healer had been able to come up with a diagnosis. Patrick asked him just two questions: "Did you change your job lately?" and "Do you drive to work now?" The man answered both in the affirmative. Then Patrick gave him the solution: if he removed his wallet from his back pocket while driving to work, his pain would stop. The bulky wallet had been cutting off the blood supply to his sciatic nerve, causing the pain in his leg.

A story of Patrick's that I particularly enjoyed recounts an incident from his eighteenth year, when his parents bought him an air ticket from Mumbai to London so he could pursue his studies there. Partying with friends, he missed his flight. He went to his aunt in Mumbai and asked her to phone his parents; but then he saw his aunt frozen in shock at the window. Following her gaze, he saw the plane he had been booked on going up in flames!

I felt a bit embarrassed to trouble Patrick with my right knee problem. I had developed a cyst in this knee at the age of twenty–four from too much running. A surgeon removed the cyst, but unfortunately had to remove some cartilage along with it; so in 2009, at age fifty-four, I was told by the sport physicians at the Sport Science Institute that I should not run any more. There was too little cartilage left in my right knee. This was a severe blow, since running is my favourite form of exercise. I had been running since the age of six, when my Dad and I would run on the beach in Hartenbos, the small town on South Africa's south coast where I grew up.

Over the course of the workshop I finally plucked up enough courage to approach Patrick with my knee problem. He was very sympathetic. "Can I have a look?" he asked. He scanned my knee with his right hand, then did some healing procedure using colours. I now know that he would probably have used sunrise orange to energise and strengthen, combined with canary yellow to build, bind, and bond. He may have finished up with electric violet, which he told us is an "all-purpose colour" with protective properties.

After this healing encounter, my knee felt warm for about an hour. Patrick told me it was fine now; I could race again! The next day my back was a little sore, as if my body was adjusting itself to the healing. A week later, I participated in an eight-kilometre trail race near Stellenbosch. It was pure bliss—and my knee and leg remained pain-free afterwards!

I have since run two more time trials and raced ten kilometres at the famous Foot of Africa race in Bredasdorp, without any problems. It seems that this man's channelling of divine energy has healed my dodgy knee! What I find really surprising are the reactions of various of my friends. Most of them do not want to admit that a miracle healed my knee.

I remember another miracle a few years back, induced by myself through a heartfelt prayer to the Divine. Again my right knee was the problem, but this time on the inside—the medial cartilage had popped out and I was on crutches. The Friday morning before I was due to facilitate one of my weekend courses at our family home in Hermanus, I went on my knees and earnestly asked that my knee please be healed so I could facilitate the workshop properly (I had six clients to attend to). I pleaded for quite a long time—and when I got up, my knee was so much better I did not need the crutches!

I can only conclude from all this that our universe is an unfathomable mystery, and that we should delight in it. Yet it is very hard for us ego-driven humans to say, "Thy will, not mine". Again, I call to mind the writings of the late Dr David Hawkins, who—like Patrick San Francesco—urges us to surrender to the will of the Divine.

The Venerable Robina Courtin, a Buddhist nun, visited South Africa a few months after Patrick's healing workshop. In a talk called "Being Your Own Therapist", she pointed out that when all goes well, we seldom question anything. It is when things do not go our way that we object, and search for answers. Instead, Ven. Robina suggested, we could accept the "good" and the "bad" as the unfolding of life and embrace everything we encounter on our life path with equanimity. This teaching seems to me very much akin to Patrick's approach: when we let go and align ourselves to the divine will, we suffer less and unravel more of the mystery of being human.

IDEAS:

ACTIONS:

Chapter 10
A Sense of Adventure

*The best way to help mankind is through the
perfection of yourself.*

—Krishnamurti

The main thing I wanted to teach my students in the Life Skills course was that each of us is unique. Each individual should find her/his own pathway to bliss—and, of course, each should take action. Students, like all of us, are responsible for looking after themselves. Waiting for things to happen rarely yields any desirable outcome.

Take another look at the list of rewards in the life skills packet in Chapter 3. As individuals, each one of us would choose different rewards. My reward, being an adventurer, is to travel. In this final chapter, I would like to share with you my trip to Rwanda to see the gorillas.

Trip to Rwanda

Based on my own experience, the best way to travel in Africa is to go with African Geographic Travel. I had previously joined them for an unforgettable trip to the Masai Mara Reserve in Kenya to see the migration of the wildebeest and the zebras. This group requires that one travel with at least one companion, so for my Rwandan trip I was fortunate that a German friend with the requisite money and time wanted to join me.

Rwanda is a small country, and the most densely populated in Africa. It is sometimes called "the country with a thousand hills". Most Rwandans are so poor that they lack running water, but they seem generally happy and very friendly. Despite the genocide in 1994 arising from conflict between

the Hutu and the Tutsi tribes, I felt safer in Rwanda than in
the Congo, where we spent a little time during our adventure.

After landing in Kigali, the main city, my German friend and I
were transported by car to Volcano Park. This park lies in the
misty highlands where Dian Fossey did her phenomenal work
with the gorillas. Room 12 in the Muhuruha Hotel in Ruhengeri
is still known as the Dian Fossey room. Sadly, Fossey's
murder has never been solved. Her best-known book, *Gorillas
in the Mist,* became a movie starring Sigourney Weaver. The
Swahili word for a white person is *mzungu*—and in Volcano
Park you can buy a T-shirt bearing the legend "Mzungu in the
Mist"!

Along with many other international gorilla trekking aspirants,
we stayed in the lovely Mountain Gorilla View Lodge. The
bungalows were spacious (especially the bathrooms!) and the
verdant gardens were full of colourful birds. At night, a porter
arrived to light a fire in the fireplace. The food was excellent.

Volcano Park is part of the Vurungu National Park, which was
founded in 1925. It straddles Rwanda, Uganda, and the
Democratic Republic of Congo. On the morning of 11
September 2015 at about 8 a.m., we gorilla trekking aspirants
gathered at the headquarters of Volcano Park. Each of us had
paid $750 for the necessary permit.

In the Rwandan part of the park, guards track ten bands of
gorillas. We were divided into groups of eight, one for each
band. The guide assigned to our group gave us an overview
and showed us a photo of the Hirwa band we were going to
see. At about 9, we started trekking through lovely, lush
jungle trees and extinct volcanoes. The helpful porters
assigned to each pair of trekkers were very skilled at
steadying us on the steep, slippery up- and downhills.

We reached our gorilla group about an hour later. Our guide
first pointed out the alpha male silverback: big, but with
gentle brown eyes. Silverbacks weigh about 200 kg, so can't
sleep in trees because they will fall out! They get their silver

mane between the ages of eight and twelve (a gorilla's lifespan is about 45 years).

Our group of eighteen gorillas—mum with suckling five-month old baby included—was enjoying a meal when we got there. In a wonderful display of "being here now", they were completely focused on gathering and eating as much of the grass, bushes, and bamboo around as possible. The gorillas were very peaceful and not aggressive at all.

On the slope where we walked in between the gorillas, awestruck and clicking away with our cameras, I was twice stung by jungle nettles—even through my long outdoor pants. I am happy to say that the uncomfortable burning sensation went away after two or three minutes.

Once the precious hour allotted to each group was up, our guide and porters led us safely back to our vehicles. What a slick and well organised business it was; I was duly impressed! By 1 o'clock we were back at the lodge, ready for another tasty buffet lunch.

On this particular trip, we also had permits to climb Mount Nyiragongo, in the Congo. This live volcano is about 50 km from the town of Goma on Lake Kivu, a big fresh water lake that is part of the Rift of Africa. Mount Nyiragongo is a spectacular stratovolcano: a characteristically cone-shaped volcano capable of particularly violent eruptions. Nyiragongo is 3470 m high, and boasts the biggest live lava lake in the world. When the volcano erupted in 2002, boiling lava destroyed half of the town of Goma before ending up in Lake Kivu, where the heat apparently wiped out all the fish.

For this adventure, I was part of a group of about twelve adventurers. At sixty, I was the oldest of the group. We started climbing the volcano at 11 a.m., accompanied by three armed guides. The climb of about 8 km is not technically difficult; it took us about five and a half hours to reach the crater's edge. The altitude got me a bit out of breath on the final stretch, but I survived the climb and luckily developed no headache.

The crater is breath-taking. Almost a kilometre in diameter, it cradles fire and boiling lava at its centre—an awesome sight, especially after it got dark. We spent a cold night in a small wooden structure (one of six structures with a tent for two inside each one), then began our descent early next morning. Getting back down took about three and half hours. Goma is a tragically poverty-stricken area, traversed via untarred roads riddled with potholes. I was really glad to get back over the border to the Rwandan side.

After this amazing trip I was left with a deepened sense of appreciation for our amazing planet, with all its beauty and its many opportunities for discovery and travel. My bucket-list wish to see the gorillas was an awesome reward!

Be Optimistic

I trust that you have enjoyed reading about my efforts to raise my students' self-esteem in the previous chapters. May it inspire you to make your life a gift to everyone you meet by uplifting them. May your acts of kindness help us as a human race to evolve to a higher plane where peace is possible.

IDEAS:

ACTIONS:

Further Exploration

Throughout this book, I've referred to various people, organisations, books, movies, documentaries, DVDs, and websites. The list below will help you find out more about any that specially interest you.

1. Mnyengeza, Vuyokazi, "Pockets of Wealth". *Sawubona*, South African Airways, June 2013, p. 81.

2. Hamilton D.R.,*"Wired for Kindness". Odyssey Magazine*, Issue 6, 2012/2013, pp. 12–14.

3. Walsh, Bryan, *"Ending the War on Fat". Time Magazine,* June 23, 2014, pp 20–27. http://time.com/2863227/ending–the–war–on–fat/

4. Williams A.R. "Shopping by the Numbers" in *National Geographic*, September 2008.

5. Africa Geographic travel packages: africageographic.com.

6. *The Animal Communicator.* DVD. Produced by Swati Thiyagarajan. 2014.

7. Baker, Natalia. *Seize the Day: A Guidebook for Changing Times*. 2014.

8. Behrens, Ken, Christian Boix, and Keath Barnes. *Wild Rwanda: Where to Watch Birds, Primates, and Other Wildlife*. 2015.

9. Bielecki, Tessa. *Wild at Heart: Radical Teachings of the Christian Mystics* (a six-CD audio set available from soundstrue.com). 2006.

10. Break Thru Institute, Cape Coral, Florida. *Pathway to Discovery*. Sue Myers. Email:brkthruseminars@aol.com

11. *Buck*, a movie produced by Julie Goldman: http://www.buckthefilm.com/goldman.htm.

12. Byrne, Rhoda. *The Power*. 2010.

13. Campbell, T. Colin. *The China Study*: *Startling Implications for Diet, Weight Loss and Long-Term Health*. Dallas: BenBella Books, 2005.

14. Chi Kung: www.max–weier.com and YouTube, *How to Practice Qigong Exercises—The Eight Key Elements of Qigong*.

15. Cohen, Ken. 2005. *The Essential Qigong Training Guide: Strong as the Mountain, Supple as Water.*

16. Comte-Sponville, André. *A Short Treatise on the Great Virtues: The Uses of Philosophy in Everyday Life.* 2002.

17. Courtin, the Venerable Robina: www.robinacourtin.com

18. Covey, Steven, *"Big Rocks"*. http://www.appleseeds.org/Big–Rocks_Covey.htm

19. Endalweni Private Game Reserve, East London, South Africa. http://www.endalweni.co.za.

20. Fossey, Dian. *Gorillas in the Mist.* 1983.

21. Gelb, Michael J. *How to Think Like Leonardo da Vinci: Seven Steps to Everyday Genius*. 1998.

22. Gilbert, Elizabeth. *Eat, Pray, Love.* 2006.

23. Gilbert, Elizabeth. *The Signature of All Things.* 2013.

24. Hamilton, David, *Why Kindness is Good For You.* London: Hay House, 2010.

25. Hawkins, David R. *Power vs. Force*. Hay House, 1995.

26. ——. *Dissolving the Ego, Realizing the Self.* 2011.

27. ——. *Letting Go: The Pathway of Surrender*. 2012.

28. Huang Po. *The Zen Teaching of Huang Po,* translated by John Blofeld. 1958.

29. Ilibagiza, Immaculee. *Left to Tell: Discovering God Amidst the Rwandan Holocaust.* 2006.

30. Khan, Hazrat Inayat. *The Alchemy of Happiness.* 1989.

31. Klarer, Elizabeth. *Beyond the Light*. 2010. (This book has been made into a film by Chris Roland, ZENHQ Film Productions.)

32. Ladinsky, Daniel. *Love Poems from God*. 2002.

33. Maharshi, Ramana. *The Spiritual Teaching of Ramana Maharshi*. 1972.

34. Mills, Billy, *Wokini: A Lakota Journey to Happiness and Self Understanding*. Hay House, 2003.

35. Nhat Hanh, Thich, *You are Here: Discovering the Magic of the Present Moment*. Boston: Shambhala Publications, 2010.

36. Parsley, Brian*, "Leading Edge". Sawubona*, June 2013, pp. 86–88.

37. Ruiz, Don Miguel. *The Four Agreements.* 1997.

38. Rumi*: Poet of the Heart*.

39. Samarpan Foundation: www.samarpanfoundation.org.

40. San Francesco, Patrick, www.lightmovement.org.

41. Tolle, Eckhart, *The Power of Now*. 1999.

42. ——. *The Illusion of Time* (DVD). 2011.

43. Wilcox, Bradley J. et al. *The Okinawa Way: How to Improve Your Health and Longevity Dramatically*. 2001.

44. Wild Coast Horseback Adventures. http://www.wildcoasthorsebackadventures.com or email Julie-anne@sunrayfarm.co.za

45. Yogananda, Sri Sri Paramahansa. *Spiritual Diary: An Inspirational Thought for Each Day*.